THE LONG
SHADOW
OF THE BUSH

By

J. Kellogg Burnham

Foreword

Verses in this book were copyrighted at different times in 2004 and 2005.

The most recent verses are at the front of the book, some relating to things still going on as the book is printed.

Other verses are presented in generally inverse chronological order, so the reader is led down the trail of successively more remote attacks on the body politic, when one hope and the next were not yet extinguished, continuing toward a golden past where the nation possessed a federal surplus, was at peace, and was looking hopefully into the new century where the candidate with the most real votes would of course become President.

The writer's views are fallible but well-intentioned, and every person is encouraged to set the record straight on any matter here touched upon, and make his correction of public knowledge.

Author's note

First published by Dog Ear Publishing
4010 W. 86th Street, Ste H
Indianapolis, IN 46268
www.dogearpublishing.net

ISBN: 1-59858-105-8
Library of Congress Control Number: 2005938653

This book is printed on acid-free paper.

Printed in the United States of America

Dedication

to the man who
hasn't made a mistake
he can think of

helpfully

kB

contents

He Wouldn't Lie to the People

Governor's Quite a Guy

Very Clean Politics

Reflections

Details Worth Mentioning

More George

He Wouldn't Lie to the People

BENNETT'S UTTER GUTTER UTTERANCE

Bill Bennett, who is a former Cabinet Minister,
and leader of thought—or the opposite—in the GOP
delivered himself of a judgment (somewhat sinister)
on the reduction of crime in the land of the free:

"If you want to reduce the crime rate, I will tell you,
stop all the Afro-American babies from being born."
This bombshell of murder aforethought
                            and hate for our national creed
(all men are equal, free, with a chance to make it)
may have startled and frightened the speaker himself, so
he added disclaimers and changes with babbling speed.
But what you have said stays said;
                    like the dead in an accident stay dead.

His remedy, or rather the mode of crime prevention
which he suggests, and then hurries and disavows,
would—in his own case—have been extremely effective,
suppressing much lawlessness and evil intention,
had *he* been throttled in his swaddling clothes.

HE GETS HIS WEEK OFF TO A SLOW START

It is Sunday, an unbelievable disaster is striking the Big Easy
the Governor says, get out if you can
and a million people do
and those who can't are stuck.
—-
The guy wants to go bike-riding but certainly not
talk to a soldier's mom waiting for him.

It is Monday and people caught by the hurricane
are dying and dead and unknown
and the people in charge of disasters
are taking their usual steps.
—-
The guy is today making sure of arrangements
to offend an important visitor from China
by withholding customary formalities of respect.

It is Tuesday and the disaster is beyond all bounds
people drown in sewage...
—-
And the guy flies away to make a speech, about
staying the course with his invasion.

It is Wednesday and no help can reach countless citizens
trapped in man-made swamps.
—-

But the guy is making another speech
and Congress is appropriating funds out of a hoard
long since emptied to the guy's favorite corporations.

It is Thursday and TV channels show clamoring hurting
people left to die, and corpses.
—-

The guy now wants to fly to the edge of the disaster
for photo ops to show he cares.

Good people, believing that help is on the way,
desperate, with their kids in filthy water, just wait.
—-

When the guy gets next to his first sample refugee
and the camera, what an inspiring hug he swings.
He can shed tears, too. See—you know he cares.

20TH CENTURY DESIGN

We Engineers, we warned you that it would take
levees designed to withstand a number four storm
in case a number four storm should come along.

But you couldn't spare us all that much money
and we had to build something, so we built
what we thought would stand up to a number three.

And then we asked for enough to reinforce for a number three
but you only okayed enough for a lick and a promise
so we spent it making channels out on the delta,

which makes it worse, but there was a lot of pipe-laying
that had to be done so the oil companies could develop
and the boats could get through, and that sort of thing.

So we reduced our plans to match the funds,
but we worried, and told you something could happen,
and did our best with what we had to work with.

And it wasn't the levees, really, but the canals
we had to cut, didn't like them one bit
but navigation required it, so there you have it.

The Bush plan next year would have cut our funding in half.
I'll bet if we were building the pyramids
we could have cut the cost by 20 percent
by skimping on the foundations, and tight management.

The same way you Bushes engineered Iraq.

PREMONITION

We Engineers have been at work on the Big Muddy
for over a century; we have straightened out curves
and put up berms and levees and bridges
for the sake of traffic, and all with great success.

And every so often we do have a tremendous flood,
so we're always providing against the next big rain
which will render the river irresistible
for it will pop whatever works we make.

See: even without any rain in the hinterland,
Katrina did in a city full of folks
and the whole town, too, and earned us quite a name.
—-
And this wasn't even the big one we're expecting,
but when we do have a specially rainy season,
thanks to everything we've done to approach perfection:

we'll be in a freshwater inland ocean, with tides;
there'll be a waterfall 200 miles across,
falling into the Gulf; and human life
will end hereabouts with foreseeable extirpation.

There isn't time to undo all we have done
before the big one, and it's too late, to start,
but give us just half of the needed appropriation
and watch us work—

SHADOWS

Tenet could tell Clinton, "No WMDs,"
not that he had any spies to verify it,
but the UN, investigating, had found none.

But later, Tenet's unimpeachable source
presumably told him what to say, and he said it.

With all his medals, Tenet would be more at ease
if he were proven guilty of incompetence
than in his role of obedient falsifier
serving the highest office with slam-dunk stuff
to excuse and justify a needless war.

And I'd bet, this would also be the case
for chief people in Security in the White House
who said what they were told to say, flat out.

And maybe it would indeed be true as well
about that incredible speech to the UN,
spoken like an honest man, although not one.

These tests of manhood and also of maidenhood
will take years to be forgot, but never expunged.

And then there's the guy who made them do it.

SCALIA-THINK

I believe in the strict construction of their words,
just what the Founding Fathers meant and said
should be the measure of our Law today.

For his owner's vote, a black is three-fifths human
and citizen, otherwise, an article of trade.
Women, their place is in the home, of course;
they don't have rights (that needs no explanation).

Schooling the young is no business of the Union;
you can spoil a first-class plowhand with a book;
sailors and tailors and whalers need no temptation;
(kids left behind can catch on by hook or crook)
but the ruling class will provide its own education.

I do believe that 230 years of growth
and change, in a changing world, don't mean a thing.
Matchlocks are good enough for our brave troops;
our Founding Fathers did not believe in airplanes,

And that good old-time religion with burning witches,
is good enough for me, with hellfire and damnation,
and to my catholic tastes, indeed delicious.

COLIN PRESENTS HIS REGRETS

My speech to the UN—could anyone forget?
that perfume vial held aloft—those WMDs
about to be found, the danger, the awful threat
that Saddam presented to a world at peace...

I excited myself, more than the people watching,
proclaiming that all must join a war to spare
the world and Iraq from the horrors that they were hatching:
our war will be peaceful, with peace that all may share.

What I said wasn't true, but even as I said it
I knew that I made it into a barefaced lie.
Tenet and I and Condi, we all knew better.
I guess we were hypnotized. I can't guess why.

Now I confess this blot upon my record,
which not all the perfumes of Arabia can cleanse,
and my share in all the killing and destruction
that followed: enlisting Brits and Poles and Finns.

But the Turks could not be bought—not on that budget—
nor the 150 nations gathered there
who had more respect for fact and truth and honor,
and not old Europe, nor people everywhere.

But hear me:
                    Loyalty is my overwhelming virtue.

And my loyalty, serving falsehood, overcame
the respect I owed to fact and common sense
and to my country, and to our Nation's name.

Blind loyalty, serving fraud and darkest mischief,
has no limit, and it respects no borders.
We generals in lustrous uniforms and tinkling medals,
we always say, "I only obeyed my orders."

I was afraid to quit.

MORAL VALUES—A CHRISTIAN

A Christian who holds his religion in his heart
judges what goes on in the marketplace
comparing it to the Sermon on the Mount.

Pat Robertson, that arrogant moral cripple,
rich and much thought of, and venomous and misguided,
spoke like the gangster he is well paid to be:

In the middle of his prayer service, he proposes:
"Let's assassinate, we have the means to waste him,
assassinate Chavez," a man in a foreign country.

"By killing him, we save another Bush war
and save another two hundred billion dollars,"
thus, praying, on a nationwide TV hookup.

And State, instead of calling it abhorrent,
shrugs and says mildly 'it's inappropriate,"
thus praising him with faint damns, because he said it!

So! Robertson speaks for Condi and the Twig...

Our puzzled Christian will hardly find the call
to murder, in his Sermon on the Mount.

MORAL VALUES—ROBERTSON

Robertson preaching on his broadcast hookup
is like any cleric in his holy madrassah
who says "My foe is against Alláh,
if you take him out you earn a rich reward,"
thus preaching murder as if in Holy Writ.

But Chavez is a legitimate national President,
by massive popular vote of majority
in a democratic state with free elections,
able at last to turn the rascals out.

That State has a fine old wealthy feudal system
where 5 percent of people own 80 percent of everything
and are therefore deathly opposed to Chavez
for doing something for 90 percent of his people
to achieve their rights, a better life, law,
medical, schools, development, hope.

Much like our revered and hated FDR
saying, "One-third of a nation
ill-fed, ill-housed, ill-clothed—
we can do better, we must, we will—"
though Wall Street hate his guts, he did so much.

And now our Wall Street too is turning the clock back
a hundred years, to the time of the Robber Barons.
It's time for all of us to face the fact,
Democracy is in mortal peril here at home
and we need to fight, to keep our country free.

MORAL VALUES—SAVE SOCIAL SECURITY

So today we say:
                              Save Social Security
                    and Save our Medicare,
strengthen the Income Tax and the Death Tax, as required.

Here, 10 percent own 60 percent of everything, and want more,
and 40 percent own hardly anything, and do the work
and languish in preventable sickness, and injury,
and death by insecticide, as is accepted
to grow cheaper crops and raise the profit margin...

and still there are coal mine fires that kill the miner,
whose life is not worth a tiny safety expense,
and coal-fired plants killing children who breathe their poison,
and the laws unenforced, that apply against these murders.

And we still have Love Canals in half the country
and oil contamination that wipes out neighborhoods
and drinking-water wells polluted and lost
so industrialists can benefit with their own neglect;
there is a law, but it is set aside,

we change the law for the forests, to their destruction
to serve a few, but to deprive the millions—
we're going the wrong way, fighting the wrong war.

The highest duty of our State is, with freedom,
the welfare of everyone, principally of the weak,
the vets, the poor, the under-employed, injured, sick, the aged.
Our Nation is wealthy, and when providing for all
it creates more wealth for all, than when it is niggardly.

Welfare and well-being and care and health, to everyone:
the finest workable ideals of a commonwealth:

And how they are despised by gangs and feudal forces!

ADVENTURE

First it was a...War to Wipe Out Terror—
Ambitious! Since he would wield terror against terror
sure that his greater terror would overcome
and wipe out terror, other than his own;
but somehow terror becomes a wildfire, spreads...

Then he switched it to a...War for Oil and Empire—
(partly because—they tried to kill my daddy)
the troops are spent on a personal vendetta
where no one threatened us, and no one opposed,
in a land that had its own fierce native terror
which, when cast down, brought hope to all its people,
that hope lost, in years of massacre and destruction.

So change again—now, War for—say it—Democracy
perhaps as a pretext for endless occupation,
imposed in impossible form by the occupier,
but half-believed by the invader and by the victim—

and all, an immense captious display of vanity
by this exponent of hypocrisy and power,
so costly, as no other rogue ever dare squander,
and endless—until we decide to make an end.

YOUR HANDS

What does it feel like, on your hands,
and around the well-manicured fingernails,
the blood of a 100 thousand persons
even their names not known to you,
killed in their homes and in their streets?
you say, to bring democracy,
delivering them from a bloody tyrant—
you say, they must be grateful.

What do you say to slide the weight
of this still endless carnage
onto the conscience of a nation
that never intended harm to other peoples
but trusted you?

How do you smooth your tone of voice
when you send our family folks to shoot,
and to get chopped and burnt and blinded
in the optional war you took a notion to?

And all the fibs it took
corrupting Colin and Condi and Congress;
and Tony, that was truly creative
(though not good enough for Old Europe
and a hundred and fifty other nations).

Those are some hands you got.

IRAQ BODYCOUNT

Says the apologist, that many thousand? Naw,
it's barely a quarter so many, estimated,
just counting our very humanitarian invasion
with its shock and awe, but rough on civilians, hot dog.

The count does go up, from the first Bush's slaughter,
and then our starving the children, with sanctions,
and if you count the extermination by Saddam
of the uprising Bush called for, and then forgot,
it does amount to an appalling number, indeed:
anyhow a whole tremendous bunch of folks killed
who never went to do us any harm.

And if you count the kill with US weapons
by Saddam, of his own people (when we said nothing)
not to mention all he did with US weapons
against Iran, aided with our technology...

You'll find we've been on the wrong side all along,
ghastly!
and not ever once to benefit our people
in dealing fair with peoples around the world,
but only to suit the purposes of our top clique.

And if you poll the Iraqis, they will agree
and add, that now we're doing worse yet,
and if we're building army bases there
when can they hope to see the last of us?

that looked-for chopper out, out of Baghdad
with people hanging from the doorhandles and the
wheels,
heroic...
we have experience doing that.

AFTERTHOUGHT

When you go to start a war,
with hidden reasons what it's for

and you've got a guarantee:
"No Casualties!"—From Chalabi!—

but Rummy runs it on the cheap—
you should look before you leap.

Gad, what drama! Land at sea
swamp all channels on TV
claim your "Mission Accompli"
and wore your AWOL flight togs—whee!

Win the war in six weeks, fast;
then lose it as the years crawl past.
How terribly wrong was Chalabi!
And you, that believed him...supposedly?

With Abu Ghraib and Occupation—
to what depths you've plunged our nation!

THE COMPASSIONATE CONSERVER

No one would, or rightly could,
call Bush a killer of babies.
Perish the savage thought.

Still, he allows all the power plants that burn coal
to pour into the air,
which belongs to all of us, and we need it to live,
tons of poisonous mercury, as much as they choose,
and unmeasured millions of sulphur and smog.

And when the brew gets too toxic even to hide
they can swap papers, and never change a thing.

This unending cascade kills thousands of us human beings,
especially the sick, and the very young
and the old folks who don't count anyhow.

But Bush, as we know, is a proud American,
a true believer, a hymn-singing, God-fearing, born again,
Christian, saved and devout, and blest:
so why would he favor the power plant people to profit
greatly
at the expense of the lives of his fellow citizens?

Why does he? He puts first things first. First.

Forget the kids, and the lakes and the woods,
and the old guys coughing themselves away.

YOU GO WITH WHAT YOU GOT

When the War Against the Taliban and Terror
is slyly switched to a War for Oil and Empire
(before you lick the Taliban or catch bin Laden)—

"then you Go with What you Got," says the civilian Chief
of Invasion and Shock-and-Awe (but not Defense),

so you take your mountain gear to use to streetfight,
your trucks good in Kabul, but deathtraps in Baghdad,
and you, you sort out the accident and error.

When the people at the top don't know their business
and show their eagerness instead of forethought
and figure it's all the same, a war's a war

and warbucks are warbucks, and you are Morituri
(Latin for MORE TOURS OF DUTY), you've done a lot,
but at tour's end, you better go, with what you got.

OUR MEN

More of our men each month come home
with dogtags jammed into their teeth
wasted and wronged beyond all knowing,
their task not done, nor never can be.

Their foe, for love of his own land,
for vengeance on his murdered kin,
for scorn of infidel, for fury
at the wasting of his home and birthright

makes of his life his offering,
to drive the Scourge forth.
                              And greater hate
hath no man, than this, that he would lay
his life down freely in this shrine of blood
a   No   No   No to the usurping power.

Yet, if the infidel withdraws,
and spares the foe's transfiguration,
they both can live, and may perhaps
do good in their surviving days.

Governor's Quite a Guy

RECALL

He came from Jugend-land to seek his fortune,
flexing his triceps, exhibiting his teeth,
and he was fairly and bountifully received,

then he appeared in all those sick B movies
and he for that was royally rewarded;
he was our favorite poster-immigrant.

And for these qualities he was selected,
by men of unconfessable intentions,
to be their hit man in shady politics.

Sacramento is badly overspent,
49 billions torn just by the Enron-ilk,
still trying to do too much with shortened means.

So put that genius in the driver's seat:
don't raise the taxes on the well-to-do,
pay workers less, cut back the schools and clinics,

Cut out the compensation for the injured
And waste no funds on the autistic and the helpless,
Oh, and close the border, that solves everything.

And still he gropes. If he escaped the Jugend
he has never cast the Jugend out of himself.
But here we share a kind regard for all.

He ought to be honorably retired, but quickly,
with many thanks for all his helpful whacks.
RECALL HIM NOW, this year, and save our State.

ARNOLD CAN WELL REFUSE

Arnold can well refuse his pay as Governor:

he gets 5 million dollars over five years

to look out for two muscle magazines

with ads that peddle snake oil to our youth,

so Arnold vetoes our law to regulate

the snake oil supplements—with one penstroke

he earns his 5 million in dirty money

and he owes nothing to California.

But boy! We sure don't owe him anything—

Except the bum's rush.

NURSES

In our 30 million West Coast busy hive of industry
most all contribute to the common good
and build the future; but there are non-producers
like Enron, and fatcats, and druggies, that drive us down
and snatch the wherewithal from all who earn it.

We choose our public servants for governance
so it should equally serve the needs of all.
Most do. Some see to their own preference
and let the public's interest hit the wall.
Sometimes we fill the top post without thinking.

Our State relies on lifetime public servants—
the Law, Safety, Health, Teachers, Nurses—
devoted all their lifetime to protecting
the delicate vital flame of life itself.

But Arnold wants fewer nurses. Working longer. For less—
no matter what happens to patients under their care;
in front of the cameras he shows them who's boss.

Would he were Grayer and more urbane, than the Arnold klutz
boasting, "Ja! In Sacramento I am kickink their buttz!"

Very Clean Politics

DUKEDOM

It seems the Duke can't hardly make ends meet
on his Congressional salary and perks
(though lately they voted themselves a handsome raise).

This is a painful topic for the Duke:
in his devotion to his public service
he is reluctant to confess to what degree

he sacrifices, so he can do what's right.
Just a boat here, a house there, a modest tip,
a campaign contribution, a widow's mite—

he must keep up appearances, to fit in
with that èlite club on Pennsylvania Avenue
where a million is provided for incidentals;

and he swabs down the deck, personally, you bet,
on that borrowed houseboat he lives on.
                              Like Huckleberry Finn
kicking the catfish bones off his raft
to make a place for *his* Duke, famous as well.

PENCHANT FOR PENSIONS

Our glamorous Mayor Golding of San Diego
was so careful with city funds that she could not spare
the coin to help payroll our Philharmonic:
she let it collapse, go bankrupt, and disappear.

But when her Party came shopping for its Convention,
enthused and inspired by the headlines and the blare,
she dug deep, but selflessly, into the Pensions
(where no one would ever suspect, or even care).

And that secret, critical wound to the Finest City
may have bailed out many a difficult circumstance:
sure we donate tickets, and baseball parks, to Pro Teams,
but our streets and our sewer lines never stand a chance.

One old gray Mayor who ain't what he used to be
just followed the hallowed precedents that he saw;
and his fifty civic benefits and improvements
just didn't prevent the working of Murphy's Law.

But on a scale of ants to elephants, compare
the misdeeds of our Congress, and our Mayor:

our nation's Congress, with all its air of purity,
seizes the cash that we pay into Social Security,
replacing with paper that reads "full faith and credit,"
that's nothing to pay with, and it will soon reach maturity:
then they squander the cash, and get still further
indebted.

But CRASH!—payback time is upon us, and—heavens—
there's no cash for paying, or even to slow the rush:
and the wastrel mainly responsible is—you know who—
but you can't use the word "responsible" with Bush.

Remember? Clinton was paying off the federal debt.

BUYERS OF VOTES

There are more buyers of votes and congressmen

in the thronging halls of Congress (with money to pay for)

than congressmen for the buying, maybe two to one,

and hardly a law gets by without their favor.

Drive out the money-changers who have made

our House of Law into a den of thieves

and let the rule of By and Of and For

the People, be enshrined again for all.

HENRY!

"Henry! What in the world are you doing in here?"
Ralph Waldo said, flustered, in his fine clothes,
to Thoreau proudly in jail, on principle;
Henry said, "Ralph, and what are you doing out there?"

And in this sorry farce of Rove's tracks
one shining principled jailbird shames them all;
the shadows of those clanging bars fall outward
on those unfettered; and she alone is free.

And what indeed are they doing, outside!
Our meritorious leaders are keeping busy
bringing destruction and shame and war and hate
though trusted to defend our country's pride.

One token sacrifice, one citizen
can call us to our senses, if we will:
let no more falsehood fool us;
                              Impeach their rule
of harm abroad to cover crime at home.

MOTIVATIONS

And now when finally the Feds have won, in court,
their $200-billion Action against Tobacco:
funds for those four hundred thousand dead of cancer
each year, and their kids and relatives and widows—

now—boy, it's time for friends to show their love:
and so the Fed does—it cuts the judgment sum
by nineteen-twentieths, to just $10 billion
without a word to all the civil victims.

And we hear an amazing silence from the White House,
and mute Gonzales, and even the RNC—
if they don't mention it, nobody'll notice, maybe,
and there's no reason anyone can see.

Silence—well silence is more than golden;
but what can they buy with whatever they took instead?
What nature of bribes could they have found so compelling
that they'd betray the four hundred thousand dead
and the living?

Reflections

PARTICIPANTS

We use this wrapping paper to pack our marble bases;
see: we have a thousand pounds of paper rolls and endrolls,
produced from Trees, which were cut and turned into mush,
digested, and rolled up again, now as paper,
rolls like tree trunks, only they are lifeless,
but at one time they were alive, growing, green, tall,
hosting the spotted owl and vole and squirrel,
which are now gone for good, too, with clearcut, and burning.

There is harm, there's death, a desert in the making
in all of this. And we have our little part in it
when we wrap our marble bases with forest body.
We're not malignant, still we've a tiny role
in the overwhelming evil work in progress
daily destroying the life system that keeps us.

And what this is printed on also exacts its cost;
but it's essential, and worth its harm, to tell us
how it destroys Nature and all who depend thereon.

DRY HISTORY

Peoples lay claim to land forevermore;
the land defines the people while they stay,
and then they scatter like evanescent shadows;
the land stays, their footprints wear away.

Long ago, able Akkadians lost their land
between the rivers, though rich in herds and harvest,
when cursed by the sky-god—never to rain again,
only drifts and banks of dust, and hills of sand.

Earlier still, a paleface tribe residing
here on the coast was driven out or killed
by a more enterprising people, abiding
the territory for lo, nine thousand years.

But when their lease was up, the Spaniards seized it
just for a moment, till overrun by people
of the south, who are in turn defeated
by gold-lusting outlanders, also temporary:

because they scorn to embrace the earth, and lose it
back to illegals who love the soil they till,
much like the unforgiving Saxon peasants
regaining their earth from bred-out Norman nobles.

One case we know: before our recent ice age
there were brave people in boats who dared the sea
and fifty thousand years ago, captured Australia;
these people loved their land and kept it free.

And some time, ten or thirty thousand later,
there were the ancient sea kings
who traced with splendid skill the barren ice
of Antarctica, and left their perfect maps
known to our present renaissance of knowledge
some centuries before our ships could make the find.

Hereafter, other humans perhaps more human
will venture across the desolate dry riverbeds
(where now we kill our salmon and foul the waters),
and marvel at an abutment, an ancient landfill,
or stumps that hint primeval forests, and ruins
left by mad awesome reluctant self-destroyers.

FORTIUS

Natural law governs the way that sentient things
get along with one another, collectively
and individually, in their pursuit of happiness.

The early bird can win the too-soon worm;
the agilest antelope escapes the slow-leaping leopard,
so both are urged to more Olympian feats,
and each test proves a winner and a loser.

Tasmanian and wise Mohican yield their ground
to the more successful predator, the christian,
though soon eclipsed in Nanking, Sudan, the West Bank
by aspirants to the title of fiercest yet.

Perhaps we'll achieve that brief superlative in Baghdad
before we pull out in shame. We must. Noblesse oblige.

IMPASSIVE

How impassively God views a tidal wave
and all the scurrying of beasts and people,
cowards heroes stoics; love panic desperation;
time flows onward evenly; they struggle; they drown;
some live; insufferable pain and loss—
this is the cold random real world at its work.

And where was He? Was that His Work? Ask not.
(The faithful marvel—He didn't lift a Finger!
to save His own, under those broken walls.)
Inscrutable are His Ways, we may not question.
It is a Warning, to fear and tremble, to bow, pray,
to mortify the flesh, and purge our sin:
our wickedness has surely brought this Trial.

The faithful nestle in the grace and comfort,
in the assurance, and the warmth, of faith
where not the least sparrow falls unnoticed,
small comfort to the sparrow, but it does count.
And they find strength, each, in secret communion
from whence they take a sense of peace and worth,
and that communion, like a sparkling symphony,
addresses each richly, but not with word or reason,

just as the eager breast assures the newborn
the world is good and made for him to suckle;
just as the wind, rounding and fattening sails,
shows to the sailor there is power to capture.

Yet comes a time, that good is gone from sight.
The howling wind blows onto reefs and crags,
and the sailor is his own chaplain and shaman
saying, as we go down with all hands—yes,
even so, like the sparrow, we are of some account.

SUDDEN STOIC

And that least sparrow, when he falls
blest with assurance and feeling brave
perceives he's really counted out,
not even counted, thrown away,
then fiercely counts himself at last;
while still his fellow sparrows pray.
And something fine is lost, each second.

LOATH WAS LOTHARIO

Bachelor -   Her wild allure—eight lovely legs—
with all her eyes she's watching you—
and you sense her message—

Ottogam -   What of thy sex?
Art thou a full-grown spider too?

Bachelor -   So suddenly your bachelor haunts
lose their appeal; your point of view
switches; incensed, you feel the taunts:
Sure I can; I will give life anew.

True, there are risks. Your wisdom wanders
—do I misjudge her?—could I be wrong?
the more you hesitate, and ponder
if to chance your future for a song.

Then again, you think—only the brave
deserve the pheromone, this way.
Who flee this challenge are the craven,
but they come back another day
in vain to yearn for that temptation...

My time is here! My lust inspires:
I shall achieve my consummation...
Now! Now—consumed!

Historian -   Not by the fires
                 of passion, but in the intimate
                 embraces of this quite charming witch:
                 loving the very mate she ate
                 in their tête-à-tête whilst they conjugate,
                 so each does serve their fondest wish.

                 Now sated in every way, at rest
                 she lulls her efficient anatomy
                 drawing those legs inside her nest
                 and justifies the fait accompli:

Ottogam -   All slay, to live. I too. I slyly tricked him!
                 Who else is half so generous with their victim?

Historian -   Thus she who dared out-spin a goddess
                 now lures with mysteries in her bodice.

TWO TOUCHED BY FATE

The shrike, that lively bird, celebrated
because it hunts the grasshopper
chewing away on the delicate rose leaf,
and catching more than it can eat at once,
impales the bounty on the nearest thorn
for its next visit, or for its ladylove
nesting nearby, to come and mercifully
put a quick end to that ungraceful squirming,
never consulting the impatient grasshopper
as to its Hobbes's choice, to be eaten now or later,
or whether 'tis better on the thorn to suffer
its outrageous fortune, or to be gobbled up
at once. It has no voice or vote nor choice
in that which mightily concerns it.
And the shrike, too, might argue its compulsion
for, like the grasshopper, it can only prey.

CORSICAN

The little Corsican (whose island people
had long fought off that great usurping power)
achieved his quittance, as the usurper's chief:
spending their men in triumphs that filled their breasts
with glory, first, and after with cannonshot;
for him each victory was twice sublime
and made him swoon for grandeur in his heart:
for of his triumph was each wretched bone a part.

Details Worth Mentioning

HUBRIS

Life there in the desert is hard always.
A poor man toils a long time for the herds
it takes, to buy a first or second wife:
for sons are the only wealth, for a man's old age.

Once having borne children, the woman has grown loose,
not prime, as the fierce desert man bargained for,
but using salt, that sears and scars, he renews her charm

proudly; he knows full well it costs him dear:
he loses both child and woman in consequence—
when her birthpains burst her body like a bomb.
-　-　-　-
The lands of the Prophet are agreed in this—
all evil-speaking infidels should be stoned
who seek to subvert our girls to secret tricks
to not have children, to be disobedient.
-　-　-　-
Our churchmouse Government likewise prohibits us,
when using health funds abroad, which we provide,
from getting out any word about abortion—
pretended keepers of morals alone decide.

Wife-riddance, with salt, is the ultimate wickedness;
so far as we keep silent, we share the blame.
When we are silenced, Pro-Life becomes Pro-Death;
the knowledge of all the Truth is all our aim.

DEMOCRACIES

Democracies don't make war on other States,
even for long-standing and severe offenses;
slow to anger, and bent on negotiating,
they find their way, through obstacles, to peace...

except when the offense is acute and irreparable,
like, having a vast petroleum potential,
and not having WMDs, to cross us up,
and starving under the blockade of the oppressor—

These are indeed intolerable provocations
and warrant shock and awe, and acre-bombs
to blot civilian cities out forever:
and rigor in dealing with the captive people.

ENTITLEMENTS

Entitlements: Fiddle de de! There won't be any.
Not for the gibbering masses, when I get through.
I have a Plan to save all the Federal Fat
from the whimpering cries of those barefaced populists.

They think that because they've paid for it twice over
they're entitled to it and can depend upon it,
they think it's still a Government of the people—
let them wake up to a new millennium.

I hold, with Coolidge, who said it very well:
'the business of this Government, is Business';
and any objector if he dares protest
we'll give him the business, too, the very best.

This way there will be ample benefits
for the Robber Barons, the Army, and the Rich,
and Congress too, as long as they behave
and something for the media, I mean TV,
but deficits as far as the eye can see.

Care for the indigent, the old, the sick—
we're not neglecting, we're transferring it
into the charge of the faith-connected charitables
where a little Federal aid is not so terrible.

What a bonanza of brand-new Born-agains
our churches will win, by having the purse-strings!
Prob'ly the biggest Revival since Savonarola,
a daily harvest of souls each suppertime.

See, my way of bringing the nation back to God:
when naked and famished, they sure will sing our psalms.

SOCIAL S'CREWITY

Seven Americans out of every ten
will wind up overage and out of jack.
Between their sixtieth year and eighty-some
there are no jobs, nor nobody fit to labor.
(So where do they go—just push them off the dock?)

We need a safer bank than all those out there.
Only the people's Government can guarantee
to hold their money throughout their working years
and hand it back—a lifesaver—when they're old.

But only this gang in power could take that cash
and spend on corporate subsidies and tax cuts
and then complain the funds are running out.
And only a special breed of cats would do that.

The working stiff becomes the special sucker:
he pays the highest garnishing on lowest wages—
the rate should be the same for every worker,
but the rate gets lower as your take goes up.

When seven Americans out of ten discover
what the Administration has in mind
there'll be a vote so vast not even their fraud
can keep these guys in office any longer.

And maybe the ancient ritual of tar-and-feathering
might help restore some honor to the rule
of oilmen buying into the highest office
and playing every citizen for a fool.

With stable guarantees, the nation prospers.
Their old feudal state, with rich and poor, and panics,
Tara and terror, and want, is gone forever.
We shall not need a second Civil War.

IT'S A DUD!

Clinton did not cancel poor Reagan's StarWars;
he let it dream along, but on the cheap,
one more holdover from the cold Cold War.

But it was the perfect toy for Bush to fall for,
and he's fed it multibillions every year:
it's about your bullet finding their speeding bullet
out in space, and kamikazzying it.

To play, you need an enemy with rockets
for you to guess where his is and where it's headed.
And then you try to make your rocket sock it.

There isn't such an enemy now, or rocket either;
but Bush can maybe create his enemy—
he's working on it, and we'll pay the bill.

When nations agree together to not engage
in projects to nuke each other, peace is served,
provided we all comply, and act together.

But when the biggest bully gets out of line,
then there's no reason for every other state
to not do likewise, so it can shoot first, with nukes.

That way lies madness, and Bush started it.

Bush aims to start the race for nukes again.
We've got ten thousand we pledged to never use.
But he will bring nukes onto us at home.

His StarWars Program is a real non-starter;
lately, this very year, two-thousand five—
we fired our target rocket, with fine telemetry,
but then our kamikaze marvel, here on the Coast,
just sat there. No liftoff. And how instructive!

If it was for real, we'd all be vaporized.

A CERTAIN FILLIP—MORE IS ALWAYS BETTER

Sure we have always furnished cigarettes
to those who choose to buy them—and why not?
Our product is a great convenience for them
   so round so firm so neat so fully packed
   so free and easy on the craving draw
   and not a cough in a ton of coffin nails.
   Indulge a certain flair—be nonchalant
light a Murad, and make money for us.

Some people happen to be a little weak
in lungs and throat and mouth and roundabout
and quite a percentage of our customers
fall by the wayside every year, disagreeably;
their families hate us. But we can bear it,
for there's a fresh crop every year, of kids
who try us out, and find it to their liking.

And every product kills—trains and bikes and pistols,
and medicines—almost as much as we do!—
but who else gives the fatal pleasure we do?
(Narcos! of course—our Aristocracy!)
But we're legit. We happily pay our taxes,
and own our judges, lawmakers, and essential others
the American Way—the Ownership Society!

WICKED TOBACCO, CRUSHED

My fiercest foes, after a ten-year battle,
win, triumph, and totally vanquish me,
and share my unholy profits—to do good works—
and thus become my fierce allies forever.

When I address the nation's tender youth
to urge them to never buy what I provide
because it's bad, with a little wink and nod,
as I am bound to do, under the judgment,
somehow it's the best promotion I ever made
and moral too, very.

I also export, because globalization
must spread worldwide such benefits of our nation,
and draw in cancer-profit without cessation
noblesse oblige, of course.

MAKING IT A DRUG ON THE MARKET

The American People of course provide the funds
for the DEA to spend multibillions abroad,
often in politico-military improprieties,
plus poisoning peasants' crops and huts, and gunfire—
solely to keep drugs out of the USA,
or so they claim. But that's a total failure.
They allege they catch maybe 20% of imports,
like King Canute sweeping the tide back with his broom.

Why even bother? How can they be so possessed?
They could spend half that pernicious wasted money
at home, rehabbing our damaged drug users
where it would do some good, and spare some lives.

And surely they could track clear to its lair
the evil US Drug Cartel, that gorges
tax-free on trillions off the traffic.

Some think there is no US Drug Cartel.
Yet the Standard Oil of coke and crack and pot
serves every selling place, including your school,
promptly supplying every kind of dope
nightly, and every hour of every day,
and collecting every debt at pistol point.

It quietly purges every breakaway
with daily hushed-up murders, in every town,
efficiently, as a Fortune Five can do.
Their former pushers never talk, from fear;
a million of them are wasting in the slammer. (At our
expense.)

Maybe the Authorities have got the goods
on the Company, but not the green light, to move.
Perhaps it has metastacized too far—
how high does it go? Who runs this country, anyhow?

The only hope—absolutely the only way out—
is what we did for Prohibition's crime wave:
we legalized the sale, and regulated it,
applied the income tax, and grade controls,
and put the Cartel in the open—no more blood money.
We start the cure—we take away their profit.

For eighty million dupes buy drugs sometime:
It's smart—it's illegal—it's fun, like cyanide.
Such popularity must be deserved—
                                And will be served.
Our moral values enshrine it at our zenith.

STAY THE COURSE

"STAY THE COURSE!" roared misguided Johnson
for his little war was a frightening botch.
And Johnson it was who finally quit,
with so terribly many dead, on his watch.

Immense evil it is to fasten a war
upon two peoples living in peace.
But Johnson feared falling dominoes more
(what nightmares rode him?) We paid the price.

"STAY THE COURSE!" urged scheming Nixon
for he had a plan to win, he said.
And Nixon too ended, abjectly quitting
with fifty—think of it—thousand dead.

"STAY THE COURSE!" argued the general:
"all it takes is a half million Grunts
and a free-fire zone halfway to hell—"
and then, then, we all quit at once.

It began with a lie, a big one,
and with lies every step of the way;
it was of course noble in purpose,
it was waged in the same old way.

We could have won them, though not by war,
with schools and friendship; for old Ho
was practical: his hero was Lincoln.
But he fought us back, blow for blow.

In Iraq, we kill, say, a hundred to one
—quite a ratio!—on folks who just get in the way
of our well-planned friendly persuasion with firepower;
if you think like Shiron that's absolutely OK.

Now "STAY THE COURSE" we again hear the yell—
for George has learned nothing from all that has passed,
he has no nightmare, no vision of hell,
and his keepers encourage him clear to the last.

CRUSADERS

Our foreign relations are candid,
transparent, and honorable too.
Why, the Coalition nearly disbanded
till our bagmen discerned what to do.

That wasn't no bribe that we offered
to encourage their troops to join,
but just an inducement, proffered
with a modest amount of coin,

all on a high moral plain
and too modest, believe me, by half,
(with a threat, too, in case they declined)
which they did, and it made the world laugh.

Now in earnest, the Coalition's cracking
(they all wish they'd held out for more);
not one of them gets any backing
from their countries, dead set against war.

But we still had a patsy in thrall,
so we say it is time to call in
all the chits and the favors, and call in
Pow! elementary force and sheer gall:

so he goes to the UN to peddle
the tale of the WMD
and the bane in his perfume bottle
which he holds up for all to see.

That's a thin and vaporous story
and somewhat more slam than dunk—
his listeners can only feel sorry:
they scarcely believe he is—sober.

That tale failed the Agency's tenets
which are fewer now than before,
and abroad, where some honor still lingers
t'was the devil to pay, and more.

Old-Europe holds out for inspectors,
and the UN must have its say.
But the Coalition is facing defections—
so we can't wait for even a day.

So we're starting a war that's unwinnable
that can end on the day we pull out
from the shambles we've made of their country
and all that we've lost in the rout.

It's fair we should bear all our losses
that are caused by our rampaging Twig
but it's hard to explain to Iraqis
why their share of the war is so big.

NEGLECT

Well of course,
we didn't have the troops enough
to cover all the danger points

and George said keep the inspectors out,
from UN, who kept tabs on all
the duly catalogued explosives

and we were mainly thinking about oil
and their jails...

So naturally, about a year later,
their oil fields, and the records,
when we come to wonder about it,
could all that hot stuff maybe fall
into the wrong hands?
and when we come to take a look
they're gone!   Golly

But what's a few hundred tons
of ultra high explosive
says Karl.

In the hands of guys so radical
they each will gladly die
to kill just one of us,
and you can't tell who they are.

It wouldn't take a hundred tons
of that ultra high stuff like plastiq
to blow a hundred thousand troops away
one by one
and fifty thousand draftees after that.

And what'll they do then
with all the rest of those high explosives?
That's *their* problem.

And ours. We're on the spot.

UNFINISHED CHAPTER

When an absolute first class killer dictator
has proved his mettle as ally for a world power
showing his usefulness with our gas and guns
practicing on his own folks, and has oil to burn,
a very solid friendship could ensue.
  (Business as usual.)

A dictator can summon our ambassadress
to consultation, at midnight, he in his tub,
to get her assurance we won't interfere in Q8.
  (That was an ambassadress in duress.)

But a feeble President can be overwhelmed by a
powerful, warlike visiting stateswoman,
so that he does interfere, in his gangling way.
  (He's been thatched.)

And probably he's going to give his lightning response:
a blitz, that takes six months, let out contracts,
get enough parking space, while the Q8 captives
expire. But that's what it takes.
  (Ah, the logistics)

Then the feeble Boss calls off his show, losing
entirely the happy moment of triumph.
But while retreating he calls for a popular revolt
to finish his unfinished job,
and watches in silence as the dictator
massacres the revolting masses.
   (Oops, he says.)

And his scion, still feebler, once crowned, turns his powers
over to schemers
who make a still greater shambles
of that country, and of ours, partly...
   (and that's treason!)

A tragedy of fools,
but so many kids starve
while the dictator buys up imaginary WMDs
with real dollars, and fools himself
into a spider hole, alas—

But stay tuned, stay the course, stay with it:
There must be worse to come.

THAT NEW CABINET

In your roundup for a cabinet
put your brand on every one;
watch for mavericks; match with caution,
and your posse will be sworn.

(Snow is in that empty space
held by a man of honest zeal
who chose to rather take his leave
than bend, at your command: "oh kneel!")

So let the harmony of the new team
echo back your wise decrees,
let no clashing thought, or banter,
break the spell—let no one sneeze.

Let no lackey's apprehension
cloud your studied nonchalance,
no unauthorized opinion
hint of possible mischance.

Let no lookout watch for icebergs
into which your ship can stray—
all the trusting folk below decks
matter less than your display.

None must doubt the perfect issue
of your mission accompli
though the facts run on as facts will;
let the bush pretend to be,
but only God can make, a tree.

FACT

What is Truth? If you ask George to tell you
Truth is what he decides it ought to be.
George likes an honest fact, that can be twisted
the way they scammed the world with WMD.

Ah, said he gaily, there won't *be* casualties.
Chalabi has guaranteed it. Dancing and flowers
will greet our happy troops on their brief visit
to Storied Baghdad, just showing off my powers.

And I had Bremer dissolve the Iraqi army—
quick victory! With a stroke of his gold pen,
told them to go on home, and take their weapons.
He says we'll never hear from them again.

Perfidious Spaniards! Backing out on me!
Merely because they hate my noble war,
don't want to be involved in bombing cities
and running prisons like Abu Ghraib.

Says George, the war is going mighty good,
as planned, except for a diehard fighting few—
but if any man is against Our Occupation
he is a terrorist, and will receive his due.

So what! If the civilian victim count
now comes to about a hundred thousand lost
and twice as many maimed, and their cities smashed—
we earn their hate. But hah, who counts the cost,

since our Crusade is imposing Democracy—
Kate Harris style—which worked quite well for me!
But I still believe just what I said at first:
No casualties! Or anyhow, none to speak of...

HE CONFESSES

God, he confesses humbly, almost shyly
wants me to be President. Hallelujah!

This raises a problem for the American voter:
endorsements are bandied about by each promoter,
but self-endorsements, claimed from a Higher Level
rarely come in, from angel or maybe devil.

But if called, by God, how can he do God's work—
betraying the people's trust, and choosing war
under false pretenses, for unconfessable aims...
it must have been Huizilopochtli, or maybe Thor?

War Gods abound, and maybe Mars or Apollo
forgot the restrictions they're obliged to follow
and whispered their admiration in his ear
so he can say, by God, what he could hear.

But God is present now in Abu Ghraib,
not on the side of the inmates, just for the babe.
And torture is blessed as legitimate Army Policy,
not morally, nor constitutionally, but Gonzalez-y.

And when God gets involved in our politics
the ugliest kind of mud is the kind that sticks;
it's not His Fault, and rarely His Intent;
but if you're devout you sure can make a dent.

TELL

If it's true the US Army
buried bodies in a deep deep trench
in Panama
to the number of three thousand—speak!

And if it's not true, deny it! But come clean
and tell the whole truth
how many bodies in what ditches
and how many at sea.

If it's only fifteen, still it's better not to hide them
and hide from the truth, shamed.

Your honor will not be restored
till you render accounts on the lives
you took or you—spared, and you tell
whatever there may be of good
that you did
to balance the atrocity of your attack
without warning
on a people who thought you a friend.

And the folks in the States
of the kids you sent to do
whatever it was that you did,
they need to know

desperately.

WHO WHO HOOOO

Who will be the Chalabi
  for George's Second Term?
who can promise him miracles
  and leave poor George to squirm?
who can sell him a Bill of Goods
  prepaid and uninspected
to a trusting, strutting quick-rich lad
  who shouldn't have been elected!

Who will be dealing the poker hand
  for George to try to play
and boosting the stakes for George to gamble
  our whole damn farm away—
and who will speak up with a steady voice
  and stop him before he blows it?
why the Secretary of State of course
  unless she's hiding in a closet.

More George

A FAMILY LEGACY

It's in the family—the old gent, in his youth
made flight school, and went on to fly in war,
and had his plane shot down, ditched it, survived,
made headlines, and went on to his career.

And so the scion becomes a weekend warrior;
he learns to fly, and he too gets shot down,
but academically; he ditches too,
and no one cares; nobody'll ever know.

Then the old guy has his war—not just Panama
but cold realpolitik with oil, that pays;
he quits his war without changing regimes—
but he invites rebellion, then betrays it.

Recklessly following in his daddy's footsteps,
the scion makes the grade, and has his war,
but is betrayed in turn by his own tanks:
survivors of his slaughter, unappreciative,
will bring grenades inside bouquets, for thanks.

Now, like when his Arbusto bust, he stands
amid the unseemly mess he has created,
hoping for Powers that Be to bail him out;
let him repent in Crawford as a sinner,
and we will beat the bushes for the winner.

GIVER

Always a wastrel and a good-time boy,
when chosen, with five solemn nods over four
by the sworn guardians of the nation's life,
to be the country's executive and guide
his first act, after his oath, was to wrench a trillion
out of the savings of the common wealth
for those who bought him, the richest of them all,
since as he said, with guileless contempt and candor,
otherwise that treasure would anyhow get spent.

Now he can play the thousand roles he dreamed
even in his cups in his secret misspent youth:
conqueror, and warrior, and now awol no longer,
mystic, all-wise, leader, forger of destiny,
spendthrift but miser, leave no child behind,
but unforgiven through the tears of humankind.

HEART'S DESIRE

Ah, it was bliss to join the happy few
the movers and shakers, in that heady time,
that flow of plenty, when everything went right
and Kenny Boy presided over Eden,
all those kazillions waiting to be cropped
and endless funds for every special use,
and every wish was granted on the spot—
oh then, to be Governor was very heaven.

And now the ultimate, an oval office,
where I can reimburse a hundredfold
those generous offerings of those special people
with forests, taxes, rules and understandings—
so much to give, but only eight short years
for emptying our nation's treasure hoard.

SON OF GEORGE

More than just born again, I have a close
and intimate direct line to the BOSS.
So all I do in serving as Earth's First Man
is thus in concert with His Master Plan.

Wholly guided am I by our Higher Father.
But the earthly one I wouldn't want to bother
about a casual matter of peace or war;
consulting on it is bound to be a bore
for the old guy; and he'd vote for peace
anyway, so I don't ask.

                      I never cease
to listen to my voices here inside,
they whisper what to do and help decide;
since I alone determine and resolve
with wisdom and panache, while playing golf,
every question of state, and world affair,
(Look on my works, ye mighty, and despair.)

I'm always right. When have I ever erred?
What though the opposition has demurred
whenever I snatch treasure for the elite
out of those silly entitlements for the masses...
My putsch will bring the whole world to my feet
(my voices say, and they are truly fascious).

REFLECTIONS WHILE LANDING AT SEA

I do not underestimate our yeomen.
They are valiant, responsible, and true.
They do the hard work, and they do it well,
choose toil and danger, for a small reward
grateful and happy, eager to go again,
and easily replaced when something happens,
and not expensive. And I talk their language,
and they think I'm a better breed than they.

Well, sure; but just the same, the fatcats look—
at me—with that exact same smirk, that I use
to butter up the tough guys for a job;
and all the piles of treasure that I give
to the Old Money who bought this chair for me,
it never quite makes us equal. 'Cause I am trash.

BREMER COMMANDS, NO LIST OF CASUALTIES

Now the invaded are dissuaded from counting their own dead,
a tally that is not congenial to the invader.
And lest the invaded feel less liberated, instead
they are encouraged to disinter their long-gone dead
(swept away by an earlier and still more evil master)
so they may feel comparatively blest.

Families are digging, with cautious shovels
seeking each, one of his own, in foul pits, in the charnel house
that was made, over time, of their country,
each one hoping, each time: this martyr is, is not—

Hopeless discoveries, reminders of their right, denied,
at least to the body of the beloved, once killed, for
the gentle task of washing the dead, and shuddering
at his raw wounds, and placing scented herbs
and consigning him to at least a chosen grave.

And, though forbidden, the invaded may too remember
their recent dead, by name, and face, and touch
whose clotting blood still cries out, for something, some debt,
some mystery unfulfilled, perhaps some error.
The freedom fighter's unresolved conundrum:
how about more killing, just keeping careful track;
Paradise waits, and more to the point
vengeance, which never slakes its thirst.

THE ADVENTURER

As though by chance, I am become the State
(thus boldly wrested from its hapless builders),
hence absolute in command, as in wisdom surely,
attested by my personal War with Terror,
melded with a vast act of filial piety
which spans the world and comes back home upon me.
My minders keep me innocent of the reek
of broken bodies as I chat with God.

My resoluteness, shaming thoughtful counsel,
empowers me to right all earthly wrongs
although I gain the hate of every nation.
I smite at random, this power of death is mine;
Behold, I am Terror. I will destroy my State.
Praise me.

HE FORGOT

He forgot his war was aimed at Terror,
with all the world supporting a war on Terror;
instead he used that warrant that we gave him
to start his long-schemed war for hydrocarbons
for those who managed to put him where he is
for business reasons.
                              Some citizens do not like it,
and the whole world despises
a man who would lay bombs and barrages
upon a city full of children and their families,
easily mangled, impossible to revive and to restore,
all for his own profit and his prospects.

PALS

Long-time pals who fall out of favor with Cyclops
get roughly handled, as they richly deserve.
Noriega's one, and sad Saddam's another;
the tales these gentle captives could beguile us with
might do themselves no favor, yet rankle the big guy,
but we hear nothing at all. And we need to.

Chalabi's not yet in the slammer, but maybe soon.
What he could tell the world would make
      Rummy rumple, and Karl rave—
it would show the top team doing part of
what we know they did.
T'would go to show
our gangster government could stand reshaping
into something we could be proud of,
like we used to.

CIVIC (NEOCON)

So—we aren't just the only Superpower,
but an Empire, in the full sanguinary sense,
with military outposts by the hundreds
on every map, in every spot of discord;
and we export three-quarters of all the arms
that ship across the world for future bloodletting,
besides what we may need where we've invaded.
And Iraq is just for practice, to keep our hand in.

We need to be more widely feared and hated—
world-wide, if we can, universally—
for our surgical bombing runs and free-fire zones,
to give more spice to our teaching Democracy
(taught by jackbooted teachers and prison guards)
to the defeated, while we strangle it at home.

OUR PRIDE

It is our shame, we choose to strike
a people only a tenth our size
still weakened from our earlier blows
and years of famine we imposed.

Still our courageous leader told
untruths to spur us to the attack:
we paralyzed their rule of law,
imposing anarchy and fear
and crime and ruin, as our gift.

We do not count the ones we maim:
children whose hands are memories
whose homes are shards and poison dust:
some of us call it nation-building.

It is our shame, that we imprison
and torture and kill their citizens
to force confession and surrender
starving and bullying and kicking and beating them.

There was a time long since when we,
unwilling to bear half these outrages
from others, revolted against King George
and made good our defiance.

But times have come full circle:
see where we stand this time.

THE DWINDLE-PLAN

We still have in this country
a bounteous resource of tough rail-splitters
and steel-drivin' men, and daredevils
who climb high over the river, building bridge,
and ride a jackhammer deep into the rock
and plow out of sight in the dustdevils
and tease tiny hardware until it whizzes.

We have more of them than we have jobs for them to do.
Their skills and manhood are of no account
when men with soft hands choose to downsize
and outsource
          and cheat
                 and bait and switch
and buy their congressmen
and make (?) more millions than they know the meaning of.

While they poison the good earth
because it's cheaper that way—
nobody makes them clean up their pollution, heavens no,
and the air becomes a stink, bringing them profit,
and the poorest kids can't breathe; who cares?
More millions are clumping together, off-shore of course.

While the schools begin to warp and drip
and fine old bridges twist and sink
and roads go down, and ghettos rot—
True, there are useful jobs for all the idle toilers;
but the money for their pay has been stolen away,
and the jobs can't get scheduled,
and grub for the workers is out of sight,
and we go down in smoke and smut.

MISSION

We do love peace and only wish
that we may give our peace to all,
even to those who can't abide
the peace we bring with tanks and bombs.

They misconstrue our loving ways
but at their peril, for we are fierce
and we have massive killing power;
we give them many Alamos
to remember.
                  They will remember each.

They wish us to go home alive
(but that is not what we intend)
and leave them with their uncounted dead
in their own land.
                  (That's a lot to ask.)

It will be long before they see
our last helicopter departing Baghdad.
We will have taught them to unite
against the invader.

ULTIMATE WITHDRAWAL

The Kurds and Sunni and Shia are finally talking
together, resolving their irreconcilables,
and the one point they all agree on completely
is to send this unwanted Superpower walking,
which outcome they all find most highly desirable.

The best part is, that the three of them get together
on a nice high-class protocol that shows us the door
sweetly and clearly and quite unanimously:
so we do have to get, proudly, at once, and hell-for-leather,
and proclaiming we didn't go pusillanimously...(but pushed.)

But if that's what we're waiting for—
Cryminys, why do we stall?
Stand not on the order of our going, but get on the ball,
so boatloads of future casualties will come home intact
in that wisest and timely historic withdrawal from Iraq.

ON THEIR WATCH

Let us re-introduce the Republic—to the Republicans:

For all they have gained, how much greater has been the loss
for them and for all of us, and for those who come after:

   —some taxes down, but the Nation has wasted its credit;

   —some laws eased, but opened to scandalous greed

   —contracts, unspeakable, gnawing the vitals of our country;

   —the strict truth, forgot in a welter of weasel words

     that dull the meaning, and slip the responsible duty;

   —torture is back, if ever it was out—

                           but now with shameful phrases,

     with blame on the low ranks and praise for generals in charge

   —shamelessness—lies exposed and still repeated,

   —we plunge into war on the helpless, with boast and pretense,

       now who will believe a Republican leader ever again?

   —there is much mean advantage yet to be had,

                           in this den of corruption,

But let us show you again the Republic,
                    when not yet besmirched.

BUSH, THE RESOLUTE

We're staying in Iraq until they all agree
on a Constitution, just like ours, which cannot be;
and as long as they shall fight against our occupation,
doubtless forever, and die for the freedom of their nation,
so long, says Bush, will be our noble war, defending
our wobbling grip on Beltway power and treasonous spending.

So, says Bush, loftily, we'll stay as long as necessary.
We should rotate our troops to visit home more often
so there'll be more kids, who'll line up to replenish
our troop strength, down the road, for Jeb.

Printed in the United States
46147LVS00007B/73-120